# Resilience for First Responders

Mental Health Strategies and Support Specifically for Firefighters, EMTs, and Police Officers

**John Diaz**

# Disclaimer

The information provided in this book is for educational and informational purposes only. While every effort has been made to ensure the accuracy and completeness of the content, the author/publisher makes no representations or warranties of any kind, express or implied, about the completeness, accuracy, reliability, suitability, or availability of the information contained herein.

The techniques, strategies, and suggestions presented in this book are based on the author's personal experiences and research. They may not be suitable for every individual or situation. Readers are advised to use their own discretion and judgment when applying any information from this book to their own circumstances.

The author/publisher shall not be held liable for any loss, injury, or damage arising from the use of the information contained in this book. Readers are solely responsible for their own actions and decisions.

Any references to specific products, services, or organizations are provided for informational purposes only and do not constitute an endorsement or recommendation. The author/publisher shall not be held liable for any consequences resulting from the use or misuse of such products, services, or organizations.

It is recommended that readers consult with qualified professionals or experts in the relevant field before making any significant decisions or taking any actions based on the information provided in this book.

By reading this book, the reader acknowledges and agrees to the terms of this disclaimer.

# Dedication

To the brave men and women who selflessly put their lives on the line every day—our firefighters, EMTs, and police officers. This book is for you. Your resilience, courage, and dedication inspire us all, and this is a small offering to acknowledge the immense mental and emotional burdens you carry in the service of others.

To your families, who stand by your side through the toughest moments, your love and support are the foundations upon which heroes are built.

Thank you for your service. May you find strength, peace, and healing.

# Table of Content

# Introduction

The nature of being a first responder means stepping into chaos when others are running away. Whether it's firefighters rushing into burning buildings, EMTs providing life-saving care in unpredictable environments, or police officers facing the unknown with every call, the demands of the job require constant physical, mental, and emotional strength. But while the visible dangers of these professions are well-known, the hidden toll on mental health often goes unspoken and untreated.

The expectation to remain strong, calm, and composed in the face of trauma has created a culture where many first responders feel they must suppress their emotions. The problem is, the stress of the job doesn't disappear at the end of a shift. Instead, it lingers, accumulating day by day, year by year. Over time, the mental strain becomes harder to manage, manifesting in ways that can erode both professional performance and personal well-being.

First responders are taught how to save lives, manage crisis situations, and protect the public. But what they often aren't given is the education or tools to protect their own mental health. This book aims to address that gap, providing a specific, practical guide to recognizing, managing, and healing from the unique mental health challenges faced by those on the front lines. There is no one-size-fits-all solution to the mental burdens of these careers, but with the right strategies, it is possible to build resilience, cope with trauma, and thrive both on and off duty.

This book isn't about generalized advice or theoretical discussions—it's about real-world solutions for the very specific issues first responders face. You've been trained to confront life-threatening situations with a clear head and quick thinking. Now, it's time to apply that same focus to your mental health. The strategies in this book will help you face the unseen battles and build a foundation of emotional resilience that will serve you for the rest of your career.

## The Unseen Battle: Mental Health in First Responders

For most people, mental health challenges are personal and hidden from public view. But for first responders, those challenges often unfold in plain sight, intertwined with the high-pressure work of saving lives and protecting the public. Firefighters, EMTs, and police officers are trained to deal with emergencies, to make split-second decisions in life-or-death situations, and to stay calm in the face of chaos. But beneath the surface, the unseen battle with mental health can be just as fierce as any physical danger encountered on the job.

The trauma of witnessing violent accidents, the stress of making life-or-death decisions, and the emotional weight of caring for those in distress take a toll. These experiences aren't isolated; they compound over years, building layers of stress that affect your mind, body, and spirit. Mental health is an issue that remains difficult to address in many first responder communities, where the culture of toughness and resilience can sometimes discourage vulnerability. This book isn't about turning first responders into something they're not; it's about recognizing that true resilience comes from acknowledging the weight of the job and learning how to carry it without collapsing.

## Why Mental Health Matters as Much as Physical Health

Mental health is often treated as secondary to physical health in first responder careers. The logic makes sense— after all, firefighters, EMTs, and police officers need to be in top physical shape to perform their duties effectively. But the truth is, mental health is every bit as critical. What good is a strong body if the mind is weighed down by trauma, anxiety, and depression?

Imagine responding to a call where you're physically capable but emotionally overwhelmed. You might be able to carry a person out of a burning building or stabilize a patient's injuries, but if the stress, fear, or emotional toll of the job isn't properly managed, the cost will eventually catch up to you. Whether it's in the form of burnout, PTSD, or even substance abuse, untreated mental health issues can and will erode the effectiveness of even the strongest first responder.

That's why this book exists—because your mental health matters just as much as your physical health. We can't expect first responders to care for others if they aren't caring for themselves. And that starts with understanding what mental health means in the context of your specific line of work.

## Breaking the Stigma: Addressing Mental Health in the Firehouse, Ambulance, and Station

There's a deep-seated stigma in the world of first responders that prevents many from seeking help for their mental health. The culture values strength, toughness, and perseverance. Admitting that you're struggling mentally can feel like admitting weakness. This stigma is deadly, leading many first responders to bottle up their emotions and avoid seeking the help they desperately need.

But we need to start looking at mental health the same way we look at physical health. If you had a broken arm, you wouldn't hesitate to get medical attention. Mental health issues like PTSD, depression, and anxiety are no different. They're injuries of the mind, and they need treatment just as urgently. Changing the narrative around mental health in firehouses, ambulances, and police stations is one of the most important steps we can take toward building a healthier, more resilient workforce.

This book aims to break that stigma by offering clear, actionable steps for managing mental health in high-stress careers. It's not about being tough or pretending nothing affects you. It's about finding real strategies to cope with the emotional and psychological challenges that come with being a first responder.

## How This Book Can Help You Build Resilience and Navigate Trauma

This book was written for you—the firefighter, the EMT, the police officer who has seen and experienced things that few others can imagine. It was written to help you navigate the mental health challenges that come with the job and to provide you with tools to build resilience, not just for today but for the long haul.

Each chapter is specifically tailored to address the unique experiences of first responders. From understanding how trauma accumulates to identifying triggers and finding healthy ways to cope, this book will offer you straightforward, practical strategies. Whether you've been on the job for decades or are just starting your career, the information in these pages is designed to be accessible and immediately useful.

This is not a general guide to mental health; it is written with your specific challenges in mind. By the end of this book, you will not only have a better understanding of your mental health but also the skills and knowledge to take control of it. You'll learn that resilience isn't about shutting off emotions or toughing it out—it's about building a support system, practicing self-care, and knowing when to seek help.

Ultimately, the goal of this book is simple: to help you be the best version of yourself, both on the job and off. The trauma and stress you face don't have to define you. With the right tools, you can navigate the toughest parts of the job and come out stronger on the other side.

# Chapter 1: The Psychological Toll of the Job

This chapter will explore the psychological cost of being a first responder. It's not just the dramatic incidents—the ones that make the news or stay in memory for years—that take a toll. It's also the daily grind, the constant exposure to stress, and the high-stakes nature of the work. We'll break down how trauma accumulates, how compassion fatigue sets in, and how it all contributes to long-term mental health challenges that need to be addressed before they spiral out of control.

## How Trauma Accumulates: Daily Exposure to Stress and Danger

Most first responders can recall a major incident that left a deep emotional scar—a mass casualty event, the death of a child, or a situation where the outcome was entirely out of their control. These moments tend to stand out, but the reality is that trauma builds up over time through repeated exposure to high-stress situations. It's not always the big events that lead to burnout or post-traumatic stress disorder (PTSD); it's the smaller, more frequent incidents that gradually chip away at mental resilience.

The very nature of first responder work ensures that there is little time to process each event before moving on to the next. You might respond to a brutal car accident in the morning, but by afternoon, you're handling a domestic violence call or rushing to a medical emergency. The brain doesn't get a chance to heal between these traumatic encounters, and this leads to what's known as cumulative trauma. Over time, the stress becomes harder to shake, and the emotional burden grows heavier.

This accumulation can manifest in a variety of ways: emotional numbness, hypervigilance, nightmares, or even physical symptoms like chronic headaches or gastrointestinal problems. But because the culture of first responders often values stoicism and toughness, acknowledging these signs is seen as a weakness. Many first responders push through, unaware that they are slowly wearing themselves down mentally. This is why understanding how trauma accumulates is so important—without addressing the ongoing psychological impact, burnout and mental health crises become almost inevitable.

In addition to the immediate stress, first responders often struggle with the aftermath of traumatic events. The human brain is not designed to witness death and destruction on a regular basis, and over time, this can lead to long-term psychological issues. PTSD, depression, and anxiety are all common among those in the profession, yet they are often ignored until they reach a breaking point. Recognizing the signs of cumulative trauma early is critical to mitigating its long-term effects.

There is also the issue of compartmentalization. First responders are experts at putting their emotions aside during an emergency. The ability to stay calm under pressure is a valuable skill, but when emotions are repeatedly shoved aside and never addressed, it becomes difficult to access them even outside of work. This emotional detachment can bleed into personal relationships and home life, leaving first responders feeling isolated and disconnected. Understanding how trauma accumulates is the first step in learning how to manage it before it causes irreparable harm.

## Compassion Fatigue: Caring for Others While Neglecting Yourself

One of the greatest challenges first responders face is the emotional drain of caring for others while neglecting their own mental health. Compassion fatigue, often referred to as "secondary traumatic stress," is a condition that arises from the emotional investment in helping others through their trauma and suffering. Over time, the constant exposure to others' pain, coupled with the high-stakes nature of the job, leaves first responders emotionally depleted and detached from their own needs.

At its core, compassion fatigue is the result of giving too much of yourself without taking the time to refill your own emotional reserves. First responders are often driven by a deep sense of duty and care, but this comes at a personal cost. Each time you respond to a call, whether it's administering CPR to a child, comforting a victim of violence, or trying to save someone who ultimately doesn't survive, you're giving a piece of yourself. It's not just physical energy that's expended—it's emotional energy as well.

As this emotional reserve is drained over time, it becomes harder to feel the same level of empathy and compassion that once came naturally. This doesn't mean you stop caring, but it does mean that the emotional toll makes it more difficult to invest in others' pain in the same way. The result is often emotional numbness, irritability, and a sense of detachment from both the job and personal life. Compassion fatigue can make it difficult to form connections with others, even loved ones, because there is simply nothing left to give.

In addition to emotional exhaustion, compassion fatigue can lead to feelings of guilt or inadequacy. First responders are trained to be problem-solvers, and when they are unable to help every person they encounter, it can lead to a sense of failure. This is especially true in situations where the outcome is beyond their control, such as losing a patient despite doing everything right. Over time, these feelings of guilt compound, further depleting mental resilience and contributing to burnout.

Addressing compassion fatigue requires a conscious effort to prioritize self-care and emotional recovery. It's not enough to just "push through" or ignore the emotional impact of the job. First responders must learn to recognize the signs of compassion fatigue early, before it becomes overwhelming. This means setting boundaries, seeking support when needed, and allowing space for emotional recovery—something that is often neglected in the fast-paced world of emergency response.

# PTSD in First Responders: Recognizing the Symptoms Early

Post-traumatic stress disorder (PTSD) is a term most people associate with combat veterans, but it is just as prevalent in the world of first responders. In fact, studies have shown that firefighters, EMTs, and police officers experience PTSD at significantly higher rates than the general population. The constant exposure to trauma, violence, and life-threatening situations creates the perfect environment for PTSD to develop.

Unlike physical injuries, PTSD doesn't always manifest immediately after a traumatic event. In many cases, the symptoms develop gradually, sometimes months or even years later. The delayed onset of PTSD can make it difficult to connect the dots between a past event and current mental health struggles. This is why early recognition of symptoms is so important. The sooner PTSD is identified, the sooner treatment can begin, and the better the long-term outcome.

PTSD in first responders can manifest in a variety of ways, including flashbacks, nightmares, anxiety, and emotional numbness. One of the most insidious aspects of PTSD is its ability to intrude on both personal and professional life. Flashbacks can occur at any moment, triggered by a sound, smell, or visual cue that brings the individual back to the traumatic event. This can make it difficult to function in daily life, both on and off the job.

Many first responders with PTSD also experience hypervigilance, which is a state of constant alertness. While this can be beneficial during emergencies, it becomes exhausting when it carries over into everyday life. Hypervigilance can make it difficult to relax or feel safe, leading to chronic anxiety and irritability. Left untreated, PTSD can also lead to substance abuse, depression, and even suicidal thoughts.

Recognizing the early signs of PTSD is critical for effective treatment. Many first responders avoid seeking help out of fear that it will affect their career or reputation. However, untreated PTSD can have far more devastating consequences. By addressing it early, first responders can regain control of their mental health and continue to serve their communities without sacrificing their own well-being.

# The Difference Between Stress and Chronic Trauma

It's important to differentiate between the normal stress of the job and chronic trauma. Stress is an inevitable part of being a first responder, but chronic trauma is something entirely different. Stress can be managed with proper coping mechanisms, but chronic trauma, left unchecked, can lead to long-term psychological damage. Chronic trauma is the result of repeated exposure to traumatic events, and it often goes unnoticed until it has already caused significant harm.

First responders often normalize their experiences, telling themselves that what they are going through is just "part of the job." But just because trauma is common in these professions doesn't mean it should be ignored. Chronic trauma affects not only mental health but physical health as well, leading to problems such as insomnia, high blood pressure, and heart disease. It also takes a toll on relationships, making it difficult to connect with loved ones or engage in meaningful social interactions.

Understanding the difference between stress and chronic trauma is essential for early intervention. While stress can be managed with strategies like exercise, relaxation techniques, and peer support, chronic trauma requires a deeper level of care, often involving therapy or other professional interventions. By recognizing the warning signs of chronic trauma, first responders can take steps to protect their mental health before it's too late.

# Chapter 2: Breaking the Stigma of Mental Health in First Responders

Despite the increasing awareness of mental health in many professions, the stigma surrounding it remains deeply ingrained in the world of first responders. Firefighters, EMTs, and police officers are expected to embody strength, resilience, and unshakable calm under pressure. The very culture of these professions often celebrates stoicism and toughness, leaving little room for emotional vulnerability. The result is a reluctance to address mental health openly, both personally and within the profession, leading many to struggle in silence.

For first responders, admitting to mental health challenges can feel like a betrayal of the qualities they believe make them effective in their jobs. But the truth is, ignoring these issues does far more harm than good. Mental health problems don't just disappear when left unaddressed; they worsen over time, leading to burnout, depression, substance abuse, or even suicidal thoughts. Breaking the stigma is not only about encouraging first responders to seek help but also about changing the culture that discourages open discussions about mental health in the first place.

In this chapter, we'll confront the stigma head-on. We'll explore why it exists, how it perpetuates itself within first responder communities, and what can be done to break down these barriers. It's not enough to acknowledge that the stigma exists; we need to understand why it's there and how to dismantle it piece by piece. The mental health and well-being of first responders depend on it.

## The Culture of Toughness: Why First Responders Are Hesitant to Seek Help

First responders are trained to put the needs of others before their own. Whether it's rushing into a burning building, performing life-saving medical procedures, or de-escalating a volatile situation, their focus is always outward. The ability to stay calm and focused under intense pressure is not just a job requirement—it's a point of pride. But this emphasis on strength and control comes with a cost. The same traits that make first responders effective in their roles can also prevent them from acknowledging their own mental health struggles.

In many first responder communities, seeking help for mental health issues is seen as a sign of weakness. There's an unspoken belief that those who can't handle the emotional toll of the job are simply not cut out for it. This culture of toughness discourages open discussions about mental health, making it difficult for individuals to admit when they're struggling. The fear of being seen as weak or incapable often keeps first responders from reaching out for the support they need.

This mindset is reinforced by the very nature of the job. In an emergency, there's no time to process emotions or reflect on the psychological impact of what's happening. First responders are trained to compartmentalize their feelings, pushing them aside to focus on the task at hand. While this ability to suppress emotions is necessary in the moment, it becomes a problem when it extends beyond the immediate crisis. Over time, the emotional weight builds up, but the culture of toughness prevents many from seeking help before it becomes overwhelming.

The reluctance to seek help is further compounded by concerns about career implications. Many first responders worry that admitting to mental health struggles will jeopardize their jobs or lead to stigmatization within their units. There's a fear of being seen as unreliable or unfit for duty, particularly in high-stakes environments where lives are on the line. This fear creates a barrier to seeking help, even when it's desperately needed.

Addressing the culture of toughness requires a fundamental shift in how mental health is viewed within first responder communities. Leaders in firehouses, EMS units, and police departments must set the tone by openly discussing mental health and encouraging their teams to prioritize self-care. Normalizing the conversation around mental health is the first step in breaking the stigma, but it requires action at every level of the profession.

## Internalized Stigma: Why It's So Hard to Admit There's a Problem

One of the most challenging aspects of breaking the stigma surrounding mental health is that it's not just an external issue—it's internal as well. Many first responders have internalized the belief that struggling with mental health is a sign of personal failure. This internalized stigma makes it even harder for individuals to seek help because they don't just fear judgment from others; they judge themselves harshly as well.

First responders are often their own worst critics. The same drive that pushes them to excel in their jobs can also lead them to set impossibly high standards for themselves when it comes to their emotional resilience. They may feel that they should be able to handle anything, and when they can't, they see it as a personal weakness. This internalized stigma is a major barrier to seeking help because it creates a cycle of self-blame and guilt.

For many, the idea of asking for help feels like admitting defeat. They may feel that they're letting down their colleagues, their families, or even the people they serve. The pressure to be "tough" and to maintain a façade of strength is immense, and it can lead first responders to ignore their mental health needs until they reach a breaking point.

To break this cycle, it's important to recognize that mental health struggles are not a reflection of personal weakness. They are a normal response to the abnormal and often horrific situations that first responders face on a daily basis. Just as no one would judge a firefighter for being injured in a fire, no one should judge a first responder for experiencing mental health challenges as a result of their work. Breaking the stigma starts with reframing how we view mental health—not as a weakness, but as a natural part of the human experience that requires care and attention.

## Peer Pressure and the "Silent Code"

The culture of silence surrounding mental health in first responder communities is often reinforced by peer pressure. There's an unspoken "code" among many first responders that discourages talking about emotions, especially in the immediate aftermath of a traumatic event. While this silence may seem like a way of coping in the short term, it often leads to long-term emotional damage.

Peer pressure plays a significant role in maintaining this silence. First responders don't want to be seen as the "weak link" in their team, and they may fear that speaking up about their mental health will cause their peers to lose trust in their ability to perform under pressure. This fear of being judged or ostracized can prevent even those who are struggling the most from seeking help. Instead, they may downplay their feelings or brush off concerns in an effort to maintain the appearance of strength.

The "silent code" also contributes to a sense of isolation. First responders may believe that they are the only ones struggling, simply because no one around them is talking about it. This lack of open communication can make it difficult to realize just how widespread mental health challenges are within the profession. When no one speaks up, it perpetuates the myth that everyone else is handling the job just fine, while the reality is that many are silently suffering.

Breaking the silent code requires a shift in peer dynamics. It's essential for first responders to create an environment where talking about mental health is not only accepted but encouraged. This starts with leadership, but it also requires peer support. When first responders begin to openly share their experiences with one another, it creates a ripple effect that makes it easier for others to do the same. Peer support groups, mental health training, and open discussions are all critical components in breaking down the walls of silence that have kept so many struggling in the dark.

## Changing the Narrative: Mental Health as a Priority, Not an Afterthought

Breaking the stigma surrounding mental health in first responder communities is not a quick fix; it requires a long-term cultural shift. Mental health must be viewed as a priority, not an afterthought, in every firehouse, EMS station, and police precinct. This means making mental health support just as important as physical health, with resources and programs in place to help first responders address their mental well-being before it reaches a crisis point.

This shift starts with leadership. Chiefs, captains, and other leaders must set the example by openly discussing mental health and encouraging their teams to take it seriously. This isn't about showing weakness—it's about demonstrating the strength it takes to acknowledge that mental health is a critical part of overall well-being. Leaders who prioritize mental health set the tone for their teams and create an environment where it's safe to seek help when needed.

In addition to leadership, policies and programs that support mental health must be put in place. Peer support programs, access to counseling, mental health training, and regular check-ins can all help create a culture where mental health is openly discussed and prioritized. It's not enough to just talk about mental health once a year or after a major event; it needs to be an ongoing conversation.

Finally, breaking the stigma requires a change in mindset among first responders themselves. It's time to let go of the outdated belief that mental health struggles are a sign of weakness. The reality is that mental health is just as important as physical health, and ignoring it doesn't make you tougher—it makes you more vulnerable. By prioritizing mental health, first responders can protect themselves from burnout, improve their performance on the job, and lead healthier, more fulfilling lives.

# Chapter 3: Identifying the Triggers

Understanding your triggers is crucial for maintaining mental health and resilience as a first responder. Each individual's experience is unique, shaped by personal history, exposure to trauma, and even the specific nature of their job. By recognizing what sets you off, you can take proactive steps to manage your emotional responses and protect your mental well-being. This chapter will delve into the various triggers that firefighters, EMTs, and police officers may encounter, offering insights into how to identify and cope with them effectively.

## What Sets You Off: Recognizing Triggers Unique to Firefighters, EMTs, and Police

Every first responder has a unique set of experiences that shape their emotional responses to different situations. Triggers can be anything from specific sounds or smells to certain types of calls that evoke past traumas. For instance, a firefighter may find that the sound of a siren brings back memories of a particularly traumatic fire, while an EMT might react strongly to the sight of a bloodied victim. These responses are rooted in the brain's complex processing of trauma and stress.

Recognizing these triggers is the first step toward managing them effectively. Self-awareness is crucial; it requires you to reflect on your experiences and how they affect your emotions and behaviors. Keep a journal to document situations that provoke strong reactions. Note the specific circumstances, your feelings at the time, and the aftermath. Over time, patterns may emerge that can help you identify your personal triggers.

In addition to personal triggers, there are shared experiences that many first responders encounter. Calls involving children, serious accidents, or violent situations can trigger emotional responses tied to the inherent dangers of the job. Understanding that these feelings are valid can help normalize your experience. You're not alone in your reactions; many of your peers may be grappling with similar emotional responses to the same types of calls.

Furthermore, workplace culture can also shape what triggers you. In environments where there's an expectation to maintain composure, any emotional response can feel inappropriate or unwelcome. This can lead to a reluctance to acknowledge your feelings, making it even more important to identify and process your triggers in a healthy way.

Recognizing your triggers allows you to anticipate emotional responses before they escalate. Instead of being caught off guard, you can develop coping strategies to manage your reactions, whether that involves deep breathing exercises, stepping away for a moment, or talking to a peer who understands what you're going through.

## The Link Between Trauma and Sensory Overload in Emergency Situations

Emergency situations are often chaotic and overwhelming, bombarding first responders with a flood of sensory information. This overload can trigger intense emotional and psychological responses, especially for those who have previously experienced trauma. The brain is wired to react to stress, and in high-pressure situations, it can become difficult to separate immediate threats from past traumas.

Sensory overload can manifest in various ways, including heightened anxiety, irritability, or a sense of being overwhelmed. For instance, the combination of loud sirens, flashing lights, and the chaotic sounds of an emergency scene can create a perfect storm of sensory input that may cause an individual to feel as if they are back in a previous traumatic situation. This response can lead to a fight-or-flight reaction, making it challenging to think clearly or respond effectively.

Understanding the connection between trauma and sensory overload is essential for managing these experiences. First responders can benefit from learning techniques to ground themselves during high-stress situations. Grounding techniques can help you focus on the present moment and regain control over your emotional state. This might include focusing on your breath, naming five things you can see, or consciously relaxing your muscles.

Additionally, it's important to recognize when the environment is becoming overwhelming and to take proactive steps to reduce sensory input when possible. This might involve stepping outside for a moment to regroup or finding a quieter space to collect your thoughts. By acknowledging the impact of sensory overload, first responders can learn to navigate these challenges more effectively.

Recognizing how trauma and sensory overload interact can empower first responders to take control of their reactions. It's not just about surviving the moment; it's about developing strategies that allow you to thrive despite the chaos. By prioritizing self-awareness and coping strategies, you can mitigate the impact of sensory overload on your mental health.

## Emotional Flashbacks: When Trauma Resurfaces in Your Work and Home Life

Emotional flashbacks can be one of the most disorienting and distressing experiences for first responders. Unlike traditional flashbacks, which may involve vivid, intrusive memories of specific events, emotional flashbacks are more subtle yet equally powerful. They can trigger intense feelings of fear, sadness, or anxiety without any clear visual cues, making it challenging to pinpoint the source of the distress.

For many first responders, these emotional flashbacks can be linked to specific situations they've encountered on the job. For instance, a call involving a serious injury may trigger a wave of emotions associated with a past incident, even if the two events are not directly related. This can lead to a cycle of distress that affects not only work performance but also personal relationships and overall quality of life.

Recognizing the signs of emotional flashbacks is essential for effective management. Common symptoms include sudden feelings of panic, emotional numbness, or difficulty connecting with loved ones. First responders may find themselves snapping at family members or feeling overwhelmed by emotions they can't fully understand. Understanding that these feelings may be rooted in past trauma can help contextualize the experience, allowing individuals to approach their emotions with compassion rather than judgment.

Developing strategies to cope with emotional flashbacks is equally important. Techniques such as mindfulness, grounding exercises, and self-soothing can help manage overwhelming emotions when they arise. Mindfulness allows you to stay present, acknowledging the flashback without becoming consumed by it. Grounding exercises, such as focusing on your breath or using tactile objects, can help bring you back to the present moment.

Additionally, seeking professional support can be invaluable in navigating emotional flashbacks. Therapists who specialize in trauma can provide tools and strategies for processing these experiences, helping to reduce their impact over time. Connecting with fellow first responders who understand the challenges can also provide a sense of community and support, reminding individuals that they are not alone in their struggles.

Understanding emotional flashbacks is a crucial step in breaking the cycle of trauma. By recognizing the signs and developing effective coping strategies, first responders can take charge of their emotional well-being, transforming distressing moments into opportunities for healing and growth.

## How Your Job Can Heighten Your Fight-or-Flight Response

The nature of first responder work inherently puts individuals in high-stakes situations that trigger the body's fight-or-flight response. This biological reaction is designed to protect you from perceived threats, but for first responders, it can become a chronic state of being. Constantly operating in this heightened state can lead to long-term physical and emotional consequences, impacting both job performance and personal life.

In emergency situations, the fight-or-flight response is essential for survival. It prepares your body to act quickly, increasing heart rate, sharpening focus, and heightening senses. However, when this response becomes habitual due to repeated exposure to trauma, it can lead to a state of chronic stress. This not only affects mental health but can also result in physical health issues, such as hypertension, digestive problems, and weakened immune function.

First responders often find themselves in situations that require immediate and intense reactions. The expectation to respond quickly and effectively can create a cycle where the body remains in a heightened state of alertness, even when the emergency has passed. This ongoing state of arousal can make it difficult to relax, impacting sleep quality and overall emotional well-being.

Recognizing the triggers that heighten your fight-or-flight response is essential for developing strategies to manage it effectively. This might involve identifying specific situations that cause a spike in anxiety or agitation. By pinpointing these triggers, first responders can develop personalized coping mechanisms to help regulate their emotional responses.

Additionally, it's crucial to establish routines that promote relaxation and recovery. Incorporating mindfulness practices, physical exercise, and adequate rest can help counteract the effects of chronic stress. Engaging in activities that bring joy and fulfillment outside of work can also serve as a buffer against the demands of the job, allowing individuals to recharge emotionally and mentally.

Creating a supportive work environment where mental health is prioritized can further mitigate the impact of the fight-or-flight response. Peer support programs, mental health resources, and open discussions about stress management can all contribute to a culture that recognizes the importance of emotional well-being in high-pressure professions.

By understanding how the job heightens the fight-or-flight response, first responders can take proactive steps to protect their mental health. This awareness, combined with effective coping strategies, can lead to improved resilience and overall well-being.

# Chapter 4: Practical Coping Strategies for the Job

In the high-stress environment of first responders, having practical coping strategies is essential for maintaining mental health and resilience. This chapter provides actionable techniques to help navigate the pressures of the job, from grounding during emergencies to building a supportive network among peers. These strategies are not only valuable for individual well-being but also contribute to overall team effectiveness and cohesion.

---

## Grounding Techniques During Emergencies

Grounding techniques are crucial for first responders faced with overwhelming situations. These strategies help bring your focus back to the present moment, allowing you to regain control over your emotional state amid chaos. By anchoring yourself in the here and now, you can make clearer decisions and respond more effectively to emergencies.

One effective grounding technique is the "5-4-3-2-1" method. This involves identifying five things you can see, four things you can touch, three things you can hear, two things you can smell, and one thing you can taste. This exercise helps shift your attention away from distressing thoughts and sensations, enabling you to reorient yourself in the environment.

Another technique is focusing on your breath. In the midst of an emergency, it's easy to become overwhelmed and forget to breathe. Taking a moment to engage in deep, intentional breathing can calm your nervous system. Inhale deeply through your nose for a count of four, hold for four, and exhale slowly through your mouth for a count of six. This practice can help lower anxiety levels, allowing you to think more clearly and respond more effectively.

Additionally, using physical anchors can be helpful. This might involve holding onto a particular object, such as a pen or a small piece of equipment, that you can concentrate on during high-stress moments. By directing your focus to this item, you can create a mental connection that helps ground you in the present, reducing feelings of panic or overwhelm.

Incorporating these grounding techniques into your routine can significantly impact your ability to manage stress during emergencies. Practicing these techniques regularly—whether during training or in lower-stress situations—can help you become more adept at using them when they matter most. Remember, grounding isn't just about surviving a moment; it's about empowering yourself to navigate challenges with resilience and clarity.

## Mental Health Breaks: What to Do When You Can't Take Time Off

First responders often face demanding schedules that make taking time off for mental health seem impossible. However, the need for mental health breaks is crucial for maintaining well-being and preventing burnout. When traditional time off isn't feasible, finding alternative ways to recharge is essential.

One effective strategy is to incorporate short, intentional breaks throughout your shift. Even five minutes of stepping away from a stressful situation can provide a mental reset. Use this time to practice deep breathing, stretch, or take a quick walk outside. Engaging in a brief change of scenery can significantly reduce stress and improve focus.

Another option is to establish "micro-breaks" during shifts. These are short, scheduled moments when you can pause, reflect, and check in with yourself. Consider using a timer to remind yourself to take these breaks regularly. During these moments, focus on your physical and emotional state. Ask yourself how you're feeling and what you need in that moment—whether it's a quick chat with a colleague, some fresh air, or a few moments of silence.

Utilizing downtime wisely can also help. If you have moments of low activity during a shift, take advantage of this time to engage in calming activities. Listen to music, meditate, or practice mindfulness techniques. These moments can serve as valuable opportunities to recharge and gather your thoughts.

It's essential to communicate with your team about the importance of mental health breaks. Creating a culture where everyone acknowledges the need for self-care can help normalize taking these breaks. When colleagues support one another in prioritizing mental health, it fosters a healthier work environment and enhances overall team performance.

Remember, even when taking a full day off isn't possible, integrating small moments of self-care into your routine can make a significant difference in your mental health. It's about finding balance and ensuring that you're not just physically present on the job, but mentally and emotionally equipped to handle the demands of your work.

## De-escalation Tactics for Stressful Encounters

First responders often find themselves in high-stress situations that require immediate de-escalation tactics. Knowing how to manage tense encounters effectively can reduce the emotional toll on both the responder and the individuals involved. De-escalation is not just a skill; it's a vital component of maintaining safety and fostering positive interactions in chaotic environments.

One key tactic is active listening. When faced with an agitated individual, giving them your full attention can make a significant difference. Use verbal and non-verbal cues to demonstrate that you are listening—nod your head, maintain eye contact, and respond with affirmations. This approach helps to calm the individual and shows them that you care about their concerns, which can diffuse their anger or anxiety.

Another effective strategy is to use a calm and steady tone of voice. Your voice can convey authority while also promoting a sense of safety. Speaking slowly and softly can help lower the tension in the situation, encouraging the other person to mirror your calm demeanor. Avoid using jargon or aggressive language, which can escalate the situation further.

Setting boundaries is also essential in de-escalation. Clearly communicate what behaviors are unacceptable while maintaining respect for the individual. For example, if someone is shouting or threatening, let them know that you're willing to listen to their concerns but only if they can speak calmly. This approach reinforces the idea that while you're there to help, certain behaviors will not be tolerated.

Lastly, knowing when to disengage is crucial. Sometimes, no matter how effective your tactics are, a situation may still escalate. Recognizing when it's time to step back, call for backup, or seek additional resources is vital for ensuring safety for all involved. This doesn't mean failure; it's a recognition of the limits of the situation and an acknowledgment of your responsibility to protect both yourself and the public.

By incorporating effective de-escalation tactics into your interactions, you can help reduce stress for both yourself and others. These strategies not only create a safer environment but also contribute to your overall mental health by minimizing exposure to high-stress encounters.

## Peer Support: Building a Network of Allies at Work

One of the most effective coping strategies for first responders is establishing a robust peer support network. In a profession where emotional experiences can often feel isolating, having allies who understand the unique challenges of the job can make all the difference. Peer support can provide validation, encouragement, and practical resources for navigating mental health challenges.

Building a peer support network starts with fostering open communication. Encourage discussions about mental health within your team, creating a culture where sharing experiences is not only accepted but encouraged. This can be as simple as initiating conversations during downtime or creating designated times for team members to share their thoughts and feelings. Normalizing these discussions helps to break down the stigma and reinforces the idea that seeking support is a sign of strength.

Consider forming a support group where team members can meet regularly to discuss their experiences and coping strategies. This structured environment allows for deeper conversations about mental health, offering a safe space to share challenges and successes. Such groups can be instrumental in building camaraderie and trust, providing a sense of belonging in a demanding profession.

Utilizing formal peer support programs, if available, can also enhance your network. Many firehouses, EMS units, and police departments have established programs to provide mental health resources and support. These programs often include trained peer supporters who can offer guidance and help individuals navigate their mental health journeys.

Finally, don't underestimate the power of one-on-one connections. Developing strong relationships with a few trusted colleagues can create a foundation of support. Make an effort to check in on each other regularly, offering a listening ear or a simple gesture of kindness. These connections can help alleviate the burden of stress and foster resilience among team members.

Creating a strong peer support network is essential for maintaining mental health in the demanding world of first responders. By fostering open communication and encouraging supportive relationships, you can build a resilient community that not only helps individuals cope with stress but also enhances overall team effectiveness.

# Chapter 5: When the Uniform Comes Off: Off-Duty Mental Health Care

For first responders, the mental demands of the job extend beyond the shift. Transitioning from the high-stress environment of emergency work to home life can be challenging, often leaving individuals feeling emotionally drained. This chapter explores strategies for off-duty mental health care, emphasizing the importance of relaxation, social support, and self-care practices.

## Why Relaxation Feels Impossible After a Shift

After a demanding shift, the expectation to unwind can feel unrealistic for many first responders. The adrenaline rush, coupled with the mental and emotional weight of the day's events, can create a lingering state of hyperarousal. This physiological response makes it difficult to relax, leading to frustration and feelings of inadequacy when trying to transition into personal time.

One reason relaxation can feel impossible is the brain's tendency to stay in a state of alertness. After facing life-and-death situations, the body remains primed for action, making it hard to switch gears. This response can be exacerbated by the nature of the job, where the need to be vigilant is constant. Understanding that this reaction is a natural consequence of your work can help normalize your experience and alleviate self-blame.

Moreover, many first responders carry the emotional weight of their experiences home. Incidents involving trauma or loss can replay in your mind, making it difficult to engage fully with loved ones or enjoy downtime. The inability to disconnect from work-related stressors can lead to feelings of isolation and disconnection from family and friends.

To counter this, developing a structured transition routine can be beneficial. This might include engaging in a short ritual after your shift, such as taking a few minutes to decompress in a quiet space, practicing deep breathing, or even taking a short walk. These intentional practices can signal to your body that it's time to shift from work mode to personal time, helping to ease the transition.

Recognizing that relaxation takes practice can also be helpful. Just as you train for physical demands of the job, you can cultivate the ability to unwind. Setting realistic expectations for relaxation can alleviate the pressure to "turn off" immediately, allowing for a gradual process of disengagement from the stress of the day.

## Creating a Mental Health Toolkit for Home

Establishing a mental health toolkit for use at home is essential for first responders. This toolkit should include strategies and resources that promote emotional well-being and help manage stress after a challenging shift. Having a personalized toolkit empowers you to take charge of your mental health, ensuring you have effective coping mechanisms at your fingertips.

Start by identifying activities that promote relaxation and joy for you personally. This might include hobbies, exercise, meditation, or spending time with loved ones. List these activities in your toolkit so you can easily refer to them when you need a mental health boost. Consider also incorporating grounding techniques and mindfulness exercises that you can practice at home.

Another essential component of your mental health toolkit is access to resources. This could include books, articles, or podcasts focused on mental health and resilience. Having this information readily available can provide valuable insights and strategies during difficult times. Additionally, consider identifying professionals or support groups that specialize in first responder mental health, making it easier to seek help if needed.

It's also important to include practical self-care items in your toolkit. This might involve stress-relief tools such as stress balls, essential oils, or guided meditation apps. Creating a physical space in your home dedicated to relaxation—complete with calming scents, comfortable seating, and soothing music—can provide a sanctuary for unwinding after a shift.

Lastly, regularly revisiting and updating your toolkit is crucial. As your needs change, so too should your strategies and resources. Make it a habit to check in with yourself about what's working and what isn't, adjusting your toolkit accordingly. This ongoing process ensures that you have the tools necessary to prioritize your mental health in a way that feels authentic and effective.

# The Importance of Family and Social Support Systems

Family and social support systems play a pivotal role in the mental health of first responders. The unique challenges of the job can create barriers to connection with loved ones, making it essential to prioritize these relationships actively. A strong support network can provide understanding, validation, and encouragement, all of which are vital for maintaining emotional well-being.

Open communication with family members about the demands of your job is crucial. Sharing your experiences can foster empathy and understanding, helping loved ones grasp the challenges you face. This dialogue can also provide a platform for discussing your emotional needs, allowing family members to support you in ways that resonate. It's important to create an environment where you feel comfortable expressing both the burdens and triumphs of your work.

Additionally, establishing boundaries between work and home life can strengthen relationships. This might involve setting aside specific times for family activities where work discussions are off-limits, allowing for focused quality time. Engaging in shared activities, whether that's cooking, exercising, or simply enjoying a movie together, can help reinforce connections and provide a much-needed break from work-related stress.

Incorporating friends into your support network is equally important. Having a circle of friends who understand the unique challenges of your profession can provide a sense of camaraderie and relief. These relationships can offer a safe space to vent frustrations, share experiences, and find solace in knowing you're not alone in your struggles. Consider organizing regular get-togethers or informal check-ins to maintain these connections.

Furthermore, exploring peer support programs within your organization can enhance your social support system. Many departments offer resources that connect first responders with trained peers who understand the emotional toll of the job. Engaging in these programs can help normalize discussions about mental health and provide additional avenues for support.

By actively nurturing family and social support systems, you can create a foundation for resilience and emotional well-being. These connections serve as a buffer against the stresses of the job, reinforcing the importance of community and shared experiences in maintaining mental health.

# Mindfulness and Self-Care for First Responders

Incorporating mindfulness and self-care practices into your routine is essential for maintaining mental health as a first responder. Mindfulness involves being fully present in the moment, allowing you to observe your thoughts and feelings without judgment. This practice can significantly enhance your emotional resilience, providing tools to cope with stress both on and off the job.

Begin by integrating mindfulness exercises into your daily routine. This could be as simple as taking a few minutes each day to focus on your breath, observing your surroundings, or engaging in mindful walking. The goal is to cultivate awareness of the present moment, helping to reduce anxiety and emotional reactivity. As you practice mindfulness regularly, you'll likely find it easier to manage stress during high-pressure situations at work.

Self-care, on the other hand, encompasses a broader range of activities that prioritize your well-being. This can include physical exercise, engaging in hobbies, spending time with loved ones, or practicing relaxation techniques. Establishing a consistent self-care routine is crucial for replenishing your energy and reducing burnout. Recognize that self-care is not a luxury; it's a necessity for sustaining your capacity to serve others.

Furthermore, consider exploring additional self-care practices, such as yoga or meditation. These practices not only promote relaxation but also enhance physical fitness and emotional resilience. Classes or guided sessions can provide structure and support as you begin to incorporate these activities into your routine.

Ultimately, prioritizing mindfulness and self-care requires intentionality. Make a commitment to set aside time each week for these practices, recognizing that your well-being is integral to your effectiveness as a first responder. By cultivating a mindset of mindfulness and actively engaging in self-care, you can navigate the challenges of your profession with greater ease and resilience.

# Chapter 6: The Role of Leadership in Mental Health

Leadership plays a pivotal role in shaping the mental health culture within firehouses, police precincts, and EMS organizations. A supportive leadership framework can significantly influence the well-being of first responders, promoting an environment where mental health is prioritized and openly discussed. This chapter explores how leadership can create positive change and foster resilience within teams.

## Firehouse and Precinct Culture: How Leadership Can Make or Break Mental Health Support

The culture within a firehouse or precinct is largely influenced by its leadership. Leaders set the tone for how mental health is perceived and addressed, directly impacting team dynamics and individual well-being. A culture that prioritizes mental health fosters openness, understanding, and support, while a toxic environment can exacerbate stress and isolation among first responders.

Leaders must actively promote a culture that values mental health as much as physical safety. This involves openly discussing mental health issues, providing resources, and encouraging team members to seek help without fear of stigma or repercussions. Leaders who model vulnerability and share their own experiences with mental health challenges can help dismantle barriers and encourage others to follow suit.

Moreover, leadership can shape the organization's policies and practices surrounding mental health. Implementing comprehensive mental health programs, providing training on recognizing and addressing mental health issues, and establishing clear protocols for accessing support can create a robust framework for well-being. These initiatives signal to team members that their mental health is a priority and that the organization is committed to their well-being.

Conversely, a lack of leadership support can create an environment where mental health issues are ignored or stigmatized. This can lead to a culture of silence, where team members feel compelled to suffer in silence rather than seek help. Leaders must recognize the significant impact their actions and attitudes have on the mental health culture within their teams and actively work to create a supportive environment.

Ultimately, leadership plays a critical role in shaping the mental health culture within first responder organizations. By prioritizing mental health and fostering an open, supportive environment, leaders can promote resilience and well-being among their teams.

## Encouraging Open Conversations About Mental Health Among Your Team

Creating an environment where open conversations about mental health are encouraged is essential for fostering a culture of support. Leaders play a crucial role in initiating these discussions and setting the expectation that mental health is a priority for the organization.

One effective strategy is to incorporate mental health topics into regular team meetings or training sessions. Discussing mental health openly reinforces the message that it is a normal part of the human experience, and it encourages team members to share their own experiences and concerns. Consider inviting mental health professionals to speak at training sessions or workshops, providing team members with valuable insights and resources.

Additionally, leaders should actively listen to their team members and validate their feelings. Encouraging an atmosphere where individuals feel safe to express their emotions can break down barriers and promote a culture of understanding. Simple gestures, such as checking in on team members or creating informal spaces for discussion, can significantly impact team morale and cohesion.

Leaders should also recognize the importance of confidentiality in these conversations. Ensuring team members feel safe sharing their experiences without fear of judgment or repercussions is crucial for fostering trust. By emphasizing that mental health discussions are private and respected, leaders can encourage more team members to engage in these conversations.

Furthermore, celebrating mental health awareness events, such as Mental Health Month, can help normalize discussions around mental well-being. Organizing team activities or informational sessions can serve as a platform for team members to share resources and support one another.

Encouraging open conversations about mental health is vital for creating a supportive culture within first responder organizations. By prioritizing these discussions, leaders can foster an environment where team members feel safe, valued, and empowered to seek help.

# Setting Up Mental Health Resources in Your Workplace

Establishing mental health resources within the workplace is a crucial responsibility for leaders. Providing accessible support options not only demonstrates a commitment to employee well-being but also equips team members with the tools they need to manage their mental health effectively.

One of the first steps in setting up mental health resources is conducting a needs assessment. Understanding the specific mental health challenges faced by your team can guide the selection of appropriate resources. This assessment can involve anonymous surveys or informal discussions, allowing team members to express their concerns and preferences regarding mental health support.

Once the needs are identified, leaders can work to implement a range of mental health resources. This might include access to counseling services, mental health hotlines, and educational materials about mental health and wellness. Additionally, creating partnerships with local mental health organizations can provide further support and resources for team members.

Providing training for supervisors and leaders on recognizing and responding to mental health issues is also essential. Equipping leaders with the knowledge and skills to identify signs of distress and offer support can create a more responsive and supportive environment. This training can empower leaders to act as advocates for their team members, helping to bridge the gap between individuals and available resources.

Furthermore, promoting awareness of these resources is vital. Regularly communicating the availability of mental health support options and encouraging team members to utilize them can help reduce stigma and increase engagement. Consider integrating mental health resource information into onboarding processes, team meetings, and workplace communications.

By proactively setting up mental health resources within the workplace, leaders can create a supportive environment that prioritizes employee well-being. These resources not only provide practical support but also demonstrate a commitment to fostering a culture of mental health awareness and resilience.

## How to Be a Mental Health Advocate as a Senior Officer

As a senior officer, your role as a mental health advocate is crucial for promoting well-being within your organization. By leveraging your position of influence, you can drive meaningful change and foster a culture that prioritizes mental health.

One of the most important steps you can take is to lead by example. Demonstrating your commitment to mental health by openly discussing your own experiences and promoting self-care practices encourages others to do the same. Your willingness to share vulnerabilities can help break down barriers and inspire team members to seek help when needed.

Advocating for mental health also involves actively supporting policies and practices that promote well-being. This could include lobbying for mental health training programs, ensuring that resources are available, or advocating for changes in organizational culture. By aligning your advocacy efforts with the needs of your team, you can create a supportive framework that empowers first responders to prioritize their mental health.

Additionally, consider establishing a mental health task force or committee within your organization. This group can serve as a platform for discussing mental health initiatives, identifying challenges, and promoting awareness. By involving team members in these conversations, you foster a sense of ownership and collaboration in addressing mental health issues.

Finally, don't underestimate the importance of collaboration with external mental health professionals. Partnering with mental health organizations can provide valuable insights and resources for your team. Bringing in experts for training sessions, workshops, or informational events can further reinforce the importance of mental health and provide practical tools for managing stress.

By embracing your role as a mental health advocate, you can drive positive change within your organization. Your leadership can help create a culture where mental health is prioritized, fostering resilience and well-being among first responders.

# Chapter 7: Seeking Professional Help

In the demanding world of first responders, the importance of professional mental health support cannot be overstated. While peer support and camaraderie are vital, there are times when the challenges faced require the expertise of trained professionals. This chapter explores recognizing the need for professional help, selecting the right therapist, understanding therapy options, and overcoming resistance to seeking treatment.

## Recognizing When You Need More Than Peer Support

Peer support is invaluable in the first responder community, providing a sense of understanding and camaraderie. However, there are moments when the challenges you face may exceed what can be addressed through peer interactions alone. Recognizing these moments is crucial for ensuring your mental well-being.

Signs that you may need professional help include persistent feelings of anxiety, depression, or overwhelming stress that interfere with daily functioning. If you find that your coping mechanisms are no longer effective, or if you're experiencing symptoms such as intrusive thoughts, flashbacks, or severe emotional distress, it may be time to seek help.

Additionally, consider the impact of your mental health on your relationships and job performance. If you notice a decline in your ability to connect with loved ones or perform your duties effectively, this can be a significant indicator that professional support is needed. Ignoring these signs can lead to further emotional turmoil and affect not only your well-being but also the safety of those you serve.

It's important to acknowledge that seeking help is a sign of strength, not weakness. The stigma surrounding mental health can create barriers to seeking professional assistance, but recognizing when you need more than peer support is essential for your overall health. Embracing the idea that seeking help is a proactive step can empower you to take control of your mental well-being.

# Choosing the Right Therapist: Finding Professionals Who Understand First Responders

Selecting the right therapist is a critical step in the journey toward mental health. For first responders, finding professionals who understand the unique challenges of the job can enhance the therapeutic experience and foster trust. Here are some key considerations when searching for a therapist.

First, look for therapists with experience working specifically with first responders or similar populations. Professionals who have a background in emergency services or have received training in trauma-informed care can provide insights that resonate with your experiences. This specialized knowledge can help create a safe space for you to explore your challenges and develop coping strategies.

Consider the therapist's approach to treatment. Different therapists may utilize various modalities, such as cognitive behavioral therapy (CBT), eye movement desensitization and reprocessing (EMDR), or mindfulness-based therapies. Familiarizing yourself with these approaches can help you determine what might be the best fit for your needs. Don't hesitate to ask potential therapists about their methods and how they align with your goals.

Additionally, the therapeutic relationship is vital for effective treatment. It's essential to feel comfortable and safe with your therapist. During your initial consultations, pay attention to how you feel in their presence. Trust your instincts—if something doesn't feel right, it's perfectly acceptable to seek out a different therapist.

Finally, consider logistics such as location, availability, and cost. Many therapists offer sliding scale fees or accept insurance, which can be an important factor in your decision. Look for a therapist who can accommodate your schedule, as regular sessions are often crucial for progress.

Finding the right therapist can take time, but it's a worthwhile investment in your mental health. By choosing a professional who understands the unique experiences of first responders, you can foster a supportive environment that promotes healing and growth.

## Therapy Options for First Responders: Cognitive Behavioral Therapy (CBT), EMDR, and Others

Therapy offers a range of approaches tailored to the unique needs of first responders. Understanding the various options available can empower you to make informed decisions about your mental health care. Among the most effective therapies for addressing trauma and stress are cognitive behavioral therapy (CBT) and eye movement desensitization and reprocessing (EMDR).

Cognitive Behavioral Therapy (CBT) is a widely used approach that focuses on identifying and changing negative thought patterns and behaviors. This therapy helps individuals recognize how their thoughts influence their emotions and actions, providing tools to challenge unhelpful beliefs. For first responders, CBT can be particularly beneficial for addressing anxiety, depression, and the impact of traumatic experiences. It offers practical strategies to cope with stress and develop healthier thought patterns.

Eye Movement Desensitization and Reprocessing (EMDR) is another effective therapy option, especially for those dealing with trauma-related symptoms. EMDR involves processing distressing memories through a structured approach that incorporates bilateral stimulation, such as guided eye movements. This technique helps individuals reprocess traumatic memories, reducing their emotional charge and allowing for healthier coping mechanisms. Many first responders have found EMDR to be a transformative approach for addressing the effects of trauma.

In addition to CBT and EMDR, other therapeutic options may be beneficial, such as mindfulness-based therapies, trauma-focused therapy, and group therapy. Mindfulness practices can help cultivate self-awareness and emotional regulation, providing valuable skills for managing stress. Group therapy can offer a sense of community and support, allowing first responders to share experiences and coping strategies in a safe environment.

Ultimately, the best therapeutic approach will depend on individual needs and preferences. Discussing your goals and concerns with your therapist can help tailor the treatment plan to suit your specific circumstances. Exploring various therapy options can empower you to take charge of your mental health and find the support that resonates with you.

## How to Navigate Resistance to Therapy in Yourself and Your Colleagues

Resistance to seeking therapy is common among first responders, stemming from various factors such as stigma, fear of vulnerability, and misconceptions about mental health treatment. Navigating this resistance is crucial for fostering a culture that prioritizes mental well-being and encourages individuals to seek the help they need.

For yourself, recognizing and addressing any reservations you may have about therapy is the first step. It's essential to acknowledge that seeking help does not reflect weakness; rather, it demonstrates a commitment to your mental health. Consider the potential benefits of therapy, such as improved emotional resilience, enhanced coping skills, and a better quality of life. Focusing on the positive outcomes can help reframe your perspective and motivate you to take the next step.

If you're facing internal resistance, take the time to educate yourself about therapy and its processes. Understanding what to expect from therapy can demystify the experience and alleviate fears. Reach out to trusted colleagues or friends who have undergone therapy; their experiences may provide reassurance and encouragement.

When it comes to colleagues who may be resistant to therapy, creating a supportive environment is key. Start by fostering open discussions about mental health within your team, emphasizing that seeking help is a normal and positive step. Share resources and personal stories to illustrate the benefits of therapy, demonstrating that it is not only acceptable but also beneficial to prioritize mental well-being.

Additionally, consider advocating for mental health training and awareness programs within your organization. Providing information and resources can help normalize discussions about therapy and reduce stigma. By promoting a culture of support, you can help create an environment where seeking professional help is embraced rather than feared.

Navigating resistance to therapy—both in yourself and among colleagues—requires patience and understanding. By prioritizing mental health discussions and providing resources, you can help foster a culture where seeking help is seen as a proactive and valuable step toward resilience and well-being.

# Chapter 8: Building Resilience Through Physical Fitness

Physical fitness is a critical component of overall well-being, especially for first responders who face unique stressors and challenges daily. Regular exercise not only strengthens the body but also plays a significant role in enhancing mental health and resilience. This chapter explores how physical fitness can boost mental health, tailor workouts to manage stress and trauma, the importance of recovery practices, and how exercise serves as a stress reliever after difficult shifts.

## How Physical Fitness Boosts Mental Health

Engaging in regular physical activity has profound effects on mental health. Exercise is known to release endorphins, neurotransmitters that promote feelings of happiness and euphoria. This natural boost can help mitigate symptoms of anxiety and depression, making physical fitness a powerful tool for first responders who often face high levels of stress.

Research indicates that exercise can reduce the body's stress hormones, such as cortisol, while simultaneously promoting the production of neurotransmitters like serotonin and dopamine, which enhance mood and overall mental well-being. For first responders, the physical demands of their job can lead to chronic stress, making it essential to incorporate regular physical activity into their routines as a preventative measure against mental health issues.

Additionally, physical fitness offers a constructive outlet for processing stress and emotional trauma. Engaging in exercise can provide a distraction from negative thoughts and feelings, allowing individuals to clear their minds and focus on their physical well-being. This shift in focus can foster a sense of empowerment and control, helping to combat feelings of helplessness that may arise from traumatic experiences.

Furthermore, participating in group workouts or team sports can strengthen camaraderie and connection among first responders. These shared experiences not only enhance physical fitness but also create a support network that can be invaluable during challenging times. The combination of physical activity and social interaction can significantly boost morale and resilience within teams, reinforcing the idea that individuals are not alone in their struggles.

Overall, building a consistent physical fitness routine can enhance mental health, reduce stress, and foster resilience. For first responders, prioritizing fitness is not just about physical strength; it's a holistic approach to managing the emotional and psychological demands of their work.

## Tailoring Your Workout to Manage Stress and Trauma

Understanding how to tailor your workout regimen to address specific stressors and trauma is vital for maximizing the mental health benefits of physical fitness. First responders can benefit from a diverse approach to exercise that incorporates various types of workouts aimed at reducing stress and promoting resilience.

Start by integrating cardiovascular exercise into your routine. Activities such as running, cycling, or swimming elevate the heart rate, promoting the release of endorphins and providing an effective way to reduce anxiety and stress. Aim for at least 150 minutes of moderate aerobic activity each week, spread across several days. This sustained effort not only improves physical health but also cultivates a sense of accomplishment and boosts mood.

In addition to cardiovascular workouts, strength training can also play a crucial role in managing stress. Lifting weights or engaging in bodyweight exercises can enhance self-esteem and confidence, which are often challenged in high-stress environments. Aim for strength training sessions two to three times a week, focusing on major muscle groups to build overall strength and resilience.

Incorporating flexibility and mindfulness practices, such as yoga or Pilates, can further enhance mental health benefits. These practices promote relaxation, mindfulness, and body awareness, making them effective tools for managing stress and processing trauma. Aim to include at least one or two sessions of yoga or stretching into your weekly routine to balance the intensity of cardio and strength training.

Finally, consider incorporating outdoor activities into your fitness regimen. Nature has a restorative effect on mental health, and spending time outdoors can provide a refreshing change of scenery. Hiking, trail running, or engaging in recreational sports in natural settings can significantly enhance mood and reduce stress levels.

Tailoring your workout to address stress and trauma requires an understanding of your personal preferences and limitations. Listening to your body and adjusting your routine accordingly can lead to a sustainable fitness practice that promotes mental resilience.

## Recovery Practices: Sleep, Hydration, and Nutrition for Mental Resilience

Physical fitness is only one component of building resilience; proper recovery practices are equally important for maximizing mental health benefits. Prioritizing sleep, hydration, and nutrition can significantly influence overall well-being and resilience for first responders.

Adequate sleep is crucial for mental health. Sleep deprivation can exacerbate stress, impair cognitive function, and heighten emotional reactivity. First responders often work irregular hours, making it essential to establish a consistent sleep schedule whenever possible. Aim for 7-9 hours of quality sleep each night, creating a relaxing bedtime routine to signal your body that it's time to rest. Consider utilizing blackout curtains, earplugs, or white noise machines to create a conducive sleep environment.

Hydration is another critical factor in maintaining mental resilience. Dehydration can negatively affect mood, cognitive performance, and overall health. Make a conscious effort to drink enough water throughout the day, especially during and after physical activity. Consider keeping a water bottle on hand during shifts to encourage regular hydration.

Nutrition plays a vital role in mental health and resilience as well. A balanced diet rich in whole foods, including fruits, vegetables, lean proteins, and healthy fats, can provide the nutrients necessary for optimal brain function. Omega-3 fatty acids, found in fatty fish, walnuts, and flaxseeds, have been shown to support cognitive health and reduce symptoms of anxiety and depression.

Consider meal prepping to ensure you have nutritious options readily available, especially during busy shifts. Focus on incorporating a variety of foods to ensure you're meeting your nutritional needs and supporting overall well-being.

By prioritizing recovery practices such as sleep, hydration, and nutrition, first responders can enhance their physical fitness efforts and promote mental resilience. These practices serve as essential foundations for maintaining optimal mental health and coping with the demands of their profession.

# Fitness as a Stress Reliever: How Exercise Helps After a Difficult Shift

After a challenging shift, physical fitness can serve as an effective stress reliever, providing a constructive outlet for processing emotions and releasing pent-up tension. Engaging in exercise post-shift can help clear the mind, promote relaxation, and enhance overall mood.

Consider incorporating a cooldown routine after your shift, which might include light stretching, yoga, or a leisurely walk. This transition period allows your body and mind to shift from the demands of work to a more relaxed state, helping to alleviate stress and promote mental clarity.

High-intensity workouts can also serve as a cathartic release after a difficult day. Engaging in activities like running, cycling, or boxing can provide a powerful means of channeling emotions and releasing built-up tension. The intensity of these workouts can lead to a state of euphoria, often referred to as the "runner's high," which can alleviate stress and promote feelings of well-being.

It's important to listen to your body and choose workouts that resonate with your emotional state. Some individuals may find solace in high-energy workouts, while others may prefer gentler practices like yoga or swimming. Ultimately, finding an exercise routine that suits your needs and preferences is crucial for maximizing the mental health benefits of physical activity.

Incorporating post-shift workouts into your routine not only enhances physical fitness but also reinforces the importance of self-care and resilience. By prioritizing fitness as a means of stress relief, first responders can create a powerful coping strategy that promotes mental well-being and emotional balance.

# Chapter 9: Managing the Mental Health of New Recruits

The transition into the world of first responders can be both exhilarating and overwhelming for new recruits. As they embark on this demanding journey, it is essential to equip them with the tools to navigate the mental challenges they will face. This chapter explores how to prepare new first responders for the mental challenges of the job, the role of mentorship in fostering a supportive culture, the importance of early mental health practices, and insights from veteran responders about what they wish they had known from the start.

---

## How to Prepare New First Responders for the Mental Challenges of the Job

Preparing new recruits for the mental health challenges of being a first responder is a crucial aspect of their training. The realities of the job can be starkly different from their expectations, and without adequate preparation, recruits may struggle to cope with the emotional demands they encounter.

A comprehensive orientation program should include discussions about the psychological impact of the job, emphasizing the types of trauma and stressors they might face. Training should cover topics such as exposure to traumatic events, the emotional toll of high-stress situations, and the potential for developing conditions such as PTSD. By presenting these challenges early on, recruits can begin to understand the importance of mental health from the outset.

Moreover, incorporating resilience training into the onboarding process can equip new responders with effective coping strategies. Techniques such as mindfulness, stress management exercises, and cognitive-behavioral approaches can help recruits build their mental resilience. Providing practical tools and strategies during training will empower them to address mental health challenges proactively as they arise.

Encouraging open dialogue about mental health is also vital. Creating an environment where new recruits feel comfortable discussing their emotions and concerns can help normalize mental health discussions. Providing access to mental health resources, such as counseling services or workshops, can further reinforce the importance of seeking help when needed.

Ultimately, preparing new recruits for the mental challenges of the job requires a multifaceted approach that combines education, practical skills, and a supportive culture. By equipping them with the right tools and knowledge, organizations can foster a healthier and more resilient workforce.

## Mentorship: Creating a Supportive Culture for New Recruits

Mentorship plays a crucial role in supporting new recruits as they navigate the complexities of their new roles. Establishing a mentorship program can create a supportive culture that not only fosters professional growth but also prioritizes mental health.

Assigning experienced first responders as mentors can provide new recruits with a reliable source of guidance and support. Mentors can share their experiences, offer practical advice, and help new hires acclimate to the demands of the job. This relationship can also provide a safe space for recruits to discuss their concerns and emotions, reinforcing the importance of mental health in the workplace.

Encouraging regular check-ins between mentors and mentees can further strengthen this relationship. These conversations can focus on the emotional challenges of the job, providing an opportunity for new recruits to express their feelings and seek advice on coping strategies. Mentors can share their own coping mechanisms and discuss the importance of seeking help when needed, thus modeling healthy behaviors for their mentees.

In addition, fostering a culture of support among peers can enhance the effectiveness of mentorship programs. Creating opportunities for team-building activities and informal gatherings can help strengthen bonds among new recruits and their mentors, promoting camaraderie and connection. This supportive network can serve as a vital resource for navigating the emotional challenges of the job.

Ultimately, mentorship is about more than just professional development; it's about creating a culture that values mental health and well-being. By fostering strong mentor-mentee relationships, organizations can help new recruits build resilience and thrive in their roles.

# Teaching New Hires the Importance of Early Mental Health Practices

Emphasizing the significance of early mental health practices is essential for new recruits to establish a strong foundation for their mental well-being. Introducing mental health practices during training can set the stage for a proactive approach to managing stress and trauma.

First and foremost, organizations should integrate mental health education into the onboarding process. Workshops or seminars focused on the importance of self-care, coping strategies, and stress management can empower new recruits to prioritize their mental health from the beginning of their careers. Providing resources and tools, such as guided meditation apps or stress management techniques, can help recruits incorporate these practices into their daily routines.

Encouraging new hires to develop healthy habits early on can also make a significant impact. This includes promoting regular physical activity, healthy eating, and sufficient sleep—all of which contribute to overall mental well-being. Organizations can facilitate this by providing access to fitness resources, nutritious meals during training, and guidance on establishing healthy sleep routines.

Moreover, teaching new recruits about the importance of seeking help when needed is crucial. Encouraging them to recognize signs of mental distress and reassuring them that seeking assistance is a strength can foster a culture of openness around mental health. Providing access to counseling services or peer support programs can reinforce this message and help new hires understand that they are not alone in their struggles.

By instilling the importance of early mental health practices in new recruits, organizations can empower them to take charge of their mental well-being and navigate the challenges of their roles with resilience and confidence.

## What Veteran First Responders Wish They Had Known from the Start

Insights from veteran first responders can provide invaluable guidance for new recruits as they embark on their careers. Understanding what experienced responders wish they had known can help shape a more informed approach to managing mental health challenges.

One common theme among veterans is the importance of prioritizing mental health early in their careers. Many express regret about neglecting their mental well-being in favor of focusing solely on job performance. New recruits should be encouraged to view mental health as a critical aspect of their overall performance, understanding that taking care of their emotional needs is just as important as physical fitness.

Veterans also emphasize the value of building strong relationships with colleagues. Developing a supportive network can provide a crucial lifeline during challenging times. New recruits should be encouraged to engage with their peers, seek mentorship, and cultivate camaraderie, recognizing that they do not have to navigate their experiences alone.

Additionally, many veterans wish they had recognized the signs of burnout and stress earlier in their careers. Understanding the warning signs of mental exhaustion can empower new recruits to take proactive measures to address their emotional health. Encouraging open discussions about mental health challenges can help normalize these conversations and promote a culture of support.

Finally, veteran responders often highlight the importance of self-care and healthy coping strategies. Many express a desire to have incorporated mindfulness practices, exercise, or hobbies into their routines earlier in their careers. New recruits should be encouraged to explore various self-care strategies and find what works best for them, reinforcing the idea that taking care of oneself is not only acceptable but necessary.

By learning from the experiences of veteran responders, new recruits can gain valuable insights into managing their mental health effectively. Fostering a culture of openness, support, and proactive mental health practices can create a more resilient and well-prepared workforce.

# Chapter 10: Managing Grief and Loss

In the line of duty, first responders often encounter traumatic events that involve death and injury, not only affecting those they serve but also deeply impacting their own emotional well-being. Grief and loss are inherent aspects of this profession, making it essential to develop strategies for coping with these challenges. This chapter explores dealing with death and injury in the line of work, coping with the loss of colleagues, processing feelings of guilt and helplessness, and practicing healthy grieving.

---

## Dealing with Death and Injury in Your Line of Work

First responders are frequently faced with death and injury, which can lead to profound emotional repercussions. The nature of their work often means that they witness the fragility of life in ways that many people never experience. Understanding how to cope with these realities is crucial for maintaining mental health.

One of the first steps in dealing with death and injury is recognizing the emotional toll it can take. It's vital for first responders to allow themselves to feel the impact of these experiences. Suppressing emotions can lead to long-term psychological issues, including PTSD, anxiety, and depression. Acknowledging that it is natural to feel sadness, anger, or confusion in response to traumatic incidents is the first step in processing these feelings.

Additionally, first responders should be encouraged to talk about their experiences with trusted colleagues or mental health professionals. Sharing stories and emotions can provide a sense of validation and support. Debriefing sessions after traumatic events can be an effective way to facilitate these conversations, allowing responders to process their feelings collectively.

Establishing a routine for self-care is also essential. Engaging in physical activity, practicing mindfulness, or participating in hobbies can help mitigate the emotional burden of dealing with death and injury. By prioritizing self-care, first responders can maintain their emotional resilience in the face of challenging experiences.

Ultimately, coping with death and injury requires a multifaceted approach that includes emotional acknowledgment, open communication, and self-care practices. By developing these strategies, first responders can foster resilience and navigate the complexities of their work more effectively.

## Coping with the Loss of Colleagues

The loss of colleagues can be one of the most challenging aspects of being a first responder. The bonds formed within these tight-knit teams are often profound, making the grief associated with losing a teammate particularly acute. Learning how to cope with this type of loss is vital for both individual and collective mental health.

First, it's essential to acknowledge the depth of the loss. Grieving the death of a colleague is a natural response, and first responders should be encouraged to express their feelings openly. This can include sharing memories, discussing the impact of the loss, and allowing space for sadness. Memorials and commemorative events can also provide a structured way to honor the fallen, helping to foster a sense of closure for the team.

It's important for teams to recognize that grief can manifest in various ways, and individuals may respond differently to loss. Some may want to talk about their feelings, while others might prefer solitude. Creating an environment that accommodates these differences is crucial. Regular check-ins and providing resources for mental health support can help ensure that everyone has access to the care they need.

Peer support can be a powerful tool in coping with the loss of a colleague. Sharing stories, offering assistance, and checking in with one another can foster a sense of community and support. Organizations should encourage this type of camaraderie, emphasizing that leaning on one another during difficult times is a sign of strength.

Finally, professional counseling should be made available to those struggling with the loss of a colleague. Mental health professionals who understand the unique challenges faced by first responders can provide valuable guidance and support during the grieving process. Encouraging individuals to seek help is essential for promoting long-term mental health and well-being.

Coping with the loss of colleagues is a complex and emotional journey, but with the right support and strategies, first responders can navigate their grief and emerge stronger together.

# How to Process Feelings of Guilt and Helplessness

Feelings of guilt and helplessness often arise for first responders when faced with death and injury. These emotions can be particularly challenging to navigate, as they may stem from the belief that they could have done more to prevent a tragedy. Understanding how to process these feelings is crucial for mental health.

First responders must recognize that guilt is a common reaction in high-stress environments. It's important to understand that these feelings often do not reflect reality. No one can control every outcome in emergencies, and acknowledging the limits of one's abilities is vital for overcoming feelings of guilt. This involves reframing negative thoughts and reminding oneself that they did the best they could given the circumstances.

Engaging in reflective practices can also help in processing feelings of guilt and helplessness. Journaling about experiences and emotions can provide an outlet for expression and may help clarify thoughts and feelings. Additionally, talking through these emotions with a trusted colleague or mental health professional can facilitate healing and promote understanding.

Furthermore, it's essential for first responders to practice self-compassion. Recognizing that they are human and that feeling guilt or helplessness does not define their worth or competence is crucial. This shift in mindset can help reduce the intensity of these feelings and foster a healthier perspective.

Lastly, focusing on what can be done moving forward rather than what has already happened is key to processing guilt and helplessness. Setting realistic goals for personal and professional growth can provide a sense of purpose and direction. Engaging in training, seeking out new knowledge, and participating in community outreach can help first responders feel more empowered in their roles.

Processing feelings of guilt and helplessness is a journey that requires time, understanding, and support. By acknowledging these emotions and working through them constructively, first responders can cultivate resilience and continue to serve their communities effectively.

# Healthy Grieving: Letting Yourself Feel Without Falling Apart

Grieving is a natural response to loss, and first responders must learn to navigate this process in a healthy way. Healthy grieving involves allowing oneself to feel the full range of emotions associated with loss while also establishing boundaries to avoid becoming overwhelmed.

One of the key components of healthy grieving is giving oneself permission to feel sadness, anger, or confusion. It's essential to understand that grief is not linear; it can ebb and flow, presenting itself in unexpected ways. Allowing oneself to experience these emotions fully, without judgment, is an essential part of the healing process.

Establishing a support system can also aid in healthy grieving. This can include friends, family, colleagues, or mental health professionals who can provide understanding and encouragement. Sharing feelings and experiences with others can create a sense of community and reduce feelings of isolation during difficult times.

Incorporating healthy coping mechanisms into the grieving process is vital. Activities such as physical exercise, creative expression through art or writing, and mindfulness practices can provide constructive outlets for processing grief. Engaging in these activities can help first responders maintain a sense of balance while navigating their emotions.

Additionally, it's important for first responders to recognize when they need to seek professional help. Grieving can sometimes become overwhelming, leading to prolonged emotional distress or difficulties in functioning. Mental health professionals can provide valuable support and guidance for those struggling to cope with their grief.

Ultimately, healthy grieving involves a delicate balance of allowing oneself to feel emotions while also seeking support and engaging in self-care. By navigating the grieving process with intention and awareness, first responders can honor their losses while continuing to thrive in their personal and professional lives.

# Chapter 11: Long-Term Mental Health Maintenance

As first responders navigate the challenges of their demanding careers, it is crucial to prioritize long-term mental health maintenance. The cumulative effects of trauma can significantly impact well-being over time, making it essential to develop sustainable strategies for ongoing mental wellness. This chapter explores recognizing the cumulative effects of trauma, creating a sustainable plan for mental wellness, managing burnout and compassion fatigue in later years, and building a fulfilling life outside the job as they prepare for life after the badge.

---

## Recognizing the Cumulative Effects of Trauma Over a Long Career

The cumulative effects of trauma are an often-overlooked aspect of being a first responder. Each traumatic event, no matter how small, can contribute to an emotional and psychological toll that accumulates over time. Understanding and recognizing these effects is vital for maintaining long-term mental health.

First responders are frequently exposed to critical incidents that can evoke intense emotions, leading to symptoms of stress or trauma. Over the years, these experiences can manifest as anxiety, depression, or PTSD. The key is to recognize that it is not just a single event but rather a series of cumulative exposures that can lead to chronic emotional distress.

It's essential for first responders to regularly assess their mental health and emotional state. This can involve self-reflection, journaling, or discussing feelings with trusted colleagues or mental health professionals. Recognizing signs of emotional exhaustion, irritability, or detachment can serve as early warning signals that the cumulative effects of trauma are taking their toll.

Additionally, organizations should implement regular mental health check-ins and training focused on the long-term effects of trauma. Educating first responders about the importance of self-care and proactive mental health maintenance can foster a culture of awareness and support. By normalizing conversations around cumulative trauma, organizations can help reduce stigma and encourage individuals to seek help before issues escalate.

Ultimately, recognizing the cumulative effects of trauma requires a commitment to ongoing self-awareness and support. By staying attuned to their mental health, first responders can take proactive steps to address the emotional impact of their experiences.

## Creating a Sustainable Plan for Ongoing Mental Wellness

Developing a sustainable plan for ongoing mental wellness is essential for first responders to thrive throughout their careers. This plan should encompass various aspects of well-being, including emotional, physical, and social health.

One of the first steps in creating this plan is to establish regular mental health check-ins. Scheduling time for self-reflection, journaling, or therapy can provide valuable opportunities to assess emotional well-being and address any concerns. First responders should be encouraged to prioritize these check-ins as an integral part of their routine.

Incorporating physical fitness into the wellness plan is also crucial. Regular exercise has been shown to have significant benefits for mental health, including reducing symptoms of anxiety and depression. Creating a structured workout routine that includes cardiovascular, strength, and flexibility training can help first responders manage stress and maintain overall well-being.

Additionally, fostering social connections is a vital component of mental wellness. First responders should be encouraged to engage in activities outside of work, building relationships with friends and family that provide emotional support. Creating opportunities for team-building or social outings can strengthen camaraderie among colleagues and promote a supportive work environment.

Finally, mindfulness and self-care practices should be integrated into the wellness plan. Techniques such as meditation, deep breathing exercises, or engaging in hobbies can help first responders manage stress and maintain emotional balance. By prioritizing these practices, first responders can cultivate resilience and enhance their mental well-being.

Creating a sustainable plan for ongoing mental wellness requires commitment and intention. By proactively addressing their mental health needs, first responders can navigate the challenges of their careers with greater resilience and fulfillment.

# Managing Burnout and Compassion Fatigue in the Later Years

As first responders progress in their careers, they may face the dual challenges of burnout and compassion fatigue. Understanding how to manage these issues is crucial for maintaining long-term mental health and job satisfaction.

Burnout is characterized by emotional exhaustion, depersonalization, and a reduced sense of personal accomplishment. It often arises from chronic workplace stress and can significantly impact an individual's performance and well-being. Compassion fatigue, on the other hand, involves the emotional strain of continually witnessing trauma and suffering in others, leading to feelings of helplessness or apathy.

To manage burnout and compassion fatigue, first responders must prioritize self-care and seek balance in their lives. This may involve setting boundaries around work hours, ensuring that time is allocated for rest and relaxation. Engaging in activities that bring joy and fulfillment outside of work can help recharge emotional batteries.

Additionally, organizations should promote a culture of support and awareness around these issues. Providing resources for mental health and wellness, as well as encouraging open discussions about burnout and compassion fatigue, can help first responders feel less isolated in their struggles. Regular training sessions focused on recognizing and addressing these challenges can empower individuals to take proactive steps to manage their mental health.

Peer support and mentorship can also play a significant role in managing burnout and compassion fatigue. Encouraging first responders to share their experiences and emotions with one another can foster a sense of community and reduce feelings of isolation. Establishing formal peer support programs can provide a structured avenue for individuals to seek help and share coping strategies.

Ultimately, managing burnout and compassion fatigue requires ongoing self-awareness, support, and proactive strategies. By prioritizing mental health and seeking help when needed, first responders can navigate the challenges of their later years with resilience and purpose.

# Building a Life Outside the Job: Preparing for Life After the Badge

Preparing for life after the badge is a crucial aspect of long-term mental health maintenance for first responders. As they approach retirement or transition to new roles, it is essential to cultivate a fulfilling life beyond their careers.

One of the first steps in this process is to identify personal interests and passions outside of work. Engaging in hobbies, pursuing education, or volunteering in the community can help first responders develop a sense of identity and purpose beyond their professional roles. Exploring new activities can also foster social connections, providing opportunities to build relationships outside of the job.

Additionally, establishing a support network is vital during this transition. Connecting with other retired first responders or community members can create a sense of belonging and provide a platform for sharing experiences and insights. Engaging in social activities or joining clubs can facilitate these connections and promote overall well-being.

Mental health professionals can also play a crucial role in this transition. Seeking counseling or support during this period can help first responders navigate the emotional challenges of leaving their careers behind. Professional guidance can provide valuable tools for managing any feelings of loss or uncertainty and help individuals establish a positive outlook for the future.

Finally, setting long-term goals for life after the badge can provide direction and motivation. Whether it's traveling, starting a new career, or dedicating time to family and community, having a clear vision for the future can help first responders embrace this new chapter with enthusiasm and purpose.

Building a life outside the job requires intentionality and commitment. By prioritizing personal growth and connection, first responders can cultivate a fulfilling life beyond their careers, ensuring long-term mental wellness and satisfaction.

# Conclusion

As we conclude this exploration of mental health strategies tailored specifically for first responders, it's crucial to underscore the importance of continued mental health work throughout your career. The realities of serving as a firefighter, EMT, or police officer involve exposure to high-stress situations and trauma that can accumulate over time. The commitment to prioritizing mental health must be ongoing, not just an afterthought or a response to crisis.

## The Importance of Continued Mental Health Work Throughout Your Career

First responders face a unique set of challenges that can take a toll on mental well-being. Recognizing that mental health is not a one-time concern but a lifelong journey is essential. Each call, each incident, adds layers to your emotional experience, creating the potential for cumulative trauma. Regular mental health check-ins, whether through self-reflection, peer discussions, or professional therapy, are vital. These practices not only help to process experiences but also build resilience and coping mechanisms for the future.

It is also important to normalize the conversation around mental health within first responder communities. By openly discussing challenges and encouraging one another to seek help, we can dismantle the stigma often associated with mental health issues. This shift in culture can lead to healthier coping strategies and a more supportive work environment, where first responders feel safe to express their needs without fear of judgment.

## Encouraging a Culture of Mental Health Awareness in First Responder Communities

Building a culture of mental health awareness starts at the top but requires participation from all levels. Leadership plays a critical role in fostering an environment where mental health is prioritized. Leaders should actively engage in mental health training, promote resources, and model self-care practices. When those in leadership positions prioritize their mental health and encourage their teams to do the same, it creates a powerful ripple effect throughout the organization.

Additionally, peer support programs can be instrumental in cultivating a culture of awareness and support. Establishing mentorship opportunities, where experienced responders guide newcomers through the emotional landscape of the job, can provide a solid foundation for resilience. Regular debriefings after critical incidents can also create safe spaces for discussing emotional responses and sharing coping strategies, reinforcing the message that mental health is a shared responsibility.

## Final Thoughts: You Are Not Alone in This Fight

As you navigate the complexities of your role, it is crucial to remember that you are not alone in this fight. Many first responders share similar experiences, and there is strength in solidarity. Engaging with colleagues, forming support groups, or participating in community discussions can foster connections that ease feelings of isolation.

When struggling, reach out. Whether it's a trusted colleague or a mental health professional, seeking help is a sign of strength. The journey towards mental wellness is ongoing, filled with ups and downs, but it is one worth pursuing. Each step you take to prioritize your mental health not only benefits you but also enhances your ability to serve and protect your community effectively.

In closing, embrace the tools and strategies discussed throughout this book. Prioritize your mental health, engage in open conversations, and build a strong support network. Together, we can cultivate a culture that values mental health and ensures that every first responder feels understood, supported, and empowered in their role.

# Glossary of Terms

**Advocacy** - The act of supporting or promoting a cause, particularly in mental health contexts.

**Altruism** - The selfless concern for the well-being of others, often seen in first responders.

**Anxiety** - A mental health condition characterized by excessive worry, fear, or apprehension.

**Burnout** - A state of emotional, physical, and mental exhaustion caused by prolonged and excessive stress.

**Burnout Prevention** - Strategies aimed at reducing the risk of burnout among individuals in high-stress occupations.

**Cognitive Behavioral Therapy (CBT)** - A type of therapy that helps individuals manage their problems by changing the way they think and behave.

**Compassion Fatigue** - The emotional strain of continually witnessing suffering and trauma in others.

**Cumulative Trauma** - The buildup of emotional and psychological stress from multiple traumatic experiences over time.

**Crisis Debriefing** - A structured process that helps individuals process traumatic experiences shortly after they occur.

**Crisis Intervention** - Immediate support provided during a mental health crisis.

**De-escalation** - Techniques used to reduce the intensity of a conflict or potential violence.

**Emotional Flashbacks** - Sudden, intense emotional reactions to reminders of past trauma, often without conscious awareness.

**Empathy** - The ability to understand and share the feelings of another person.

**Exposure Therapy** - A psychological treatment that helps individuals confront their fears in a controlled environment.

**Grounding Techniques** - Strategies that help individuals stay connected to the present moment and manage overwhelming emotions.

**Mental Health Toolkit** - A collection of strategies and resources for maintaining mental wellness.

**Mindfulness** - The practice of being fully present and engaged in the current moment, without judgment.

**Peer Support** - Emotional and practical assistance provided by colleagues who share similar experiences.

**Post-Traumatic Stress Disorder (PTSD)** - A mental health condition triggered by experiencing or witnessing a traumatic event.

**Recovery** - The process of regaining mental and emotional well-being after experiencing trauma or stress.

**Resilience** - The ability to recover from adversity and adapt to challenging situations.

**Self-Care** - Activities and practices that promote personal well-being and mental health.

**Sleep Hygiene** - Practices that contribute to the quality of sleep and overall health.

**Social Support** - Emotional and practical assistance received from family, friends, and community members.

**Stress Management** - Techniques and strategies used to control stress levels and enhance well-being.

**Therapeutic Alliance** - The relationship between a therapist and client that promotes positive therapeutic outcomes.

**Trauma-Informed Care** - An approach that recognizes the impact of trauma on individuals and seeks to provide supportive environments.

**Vicarious Trauma** - The emotional impact experienced by individuals who are indirectly exposed to trauma through their work.

**Wellness Check-Ins** - Regular assessments of an individual's mental health and emotional state.

**Work-Life Balance** - The equilibrium between professional responsibilities and personal life.

**Workplace Wellness Programs** - Initiatives designed to improve employee health and reduce stress in the workplace.

**Holistic Health** - An approach that considers the whole person—body, mind, and spirit—in promoting health and wellness.

**Coping Strategies** - Techniques that individuals use to manage stress and difficult emotions.

**Emotional Regulation** - The ability to monitor and respond to one's emotional experiences in a healthy manner.

**Intervention** - Actions taken to improve a situation, particularly in mental health support.

**Neuroscience** - The study of the nervous system and its impact on behavior and mental processes.

**Occupational Stress** - Stress related to one's job, often exacerbated in high-pressure roles like first responders.

**Psychoeducation** - Education that provides individuals with information about mental health and coping strategies.

**Risk Factors** - Conditions or variables that increase the likelihood of developing mental health issues.

**Social Isolation** - A lack of social connections that can lead to feelings of loneliness and distress.

**Support Groups** - Gatherings of individuals sharing similar experiences, offering mutual emotional support.

**Survivor's Guilt** - A feeling of guilt experienced by individuals who survive a traumatic event when others do not.

**Transitional Support** - Assistance provided to individuals during significant life changes, such as retirement from first responder roles.

**Veteran Resilience** - The ability of experienced first responders to adapt and cope with ongoing challenges in their careers.

# Did You Enjoy This Book?

Dear Reader,

I hope this message finds you well. I wanted to take a moment to express my sincere gratitude for choosing to read **Resilience for First Responders: Mental Health Strategies and Support Specifically for Firefighters, EMTs, and Police Officers**. It means the world to me that you've invested your time and trust in my work.

If you found *Resilience for First Responders* enjoyable and valuable, I would be immensely grateful if you could spare a few moments to leave a review on Amazon, Goodreads, etc. Your feedback not only helps other readers discover the book but also provides valuable insights for me as an author.

Whether it's a brief comment about what you liked most, how the book impacted you, or simply your overall impression, your review would make a significant difference. Your honest opinion is invaluable in helping me grow as a writer and in reaching more readers.

Thank you so much for your support and for being a part of this journey with me. Your reviews truly mean the world to me.

Warmest regards,

*John Diaz*

**Three Isles Publishing**

# About the Author

John Diaz is a seasoned first responder with over 20 years of experience as a firefighter and EMT. Throughout his career, John has witnessed the toughest challenges that come with serving on the front lines—facing trauma, loss, and the mental toll that accompanies the daily pressures of the job. His personal struggles with anxiety, depression, and PTSD have driven his passion for mental health advocacy within the first responder community.

John's firsthand experiences with the emotional and psychological demands of his profession have led him to become a vocal proponent for breaking the stigma around mental health in fire stations, ambulances, and police precincts. In *Resilience for First Responders*, John shares the tools, strategies, and support systems that have helped him and countless others not only survive but thrive in their roles.

John lives with his family, where he continues his work as a first responder, educator, and advocate for mental wellness. When he's not on duty, he dedicates his time to mentoring and providing resources for first responders dealing with the invisible wounds of their service. His mission is simple: to ensure that no one in his profession has to face their mental health struggles alone.

9 798340 219930